September Swim

Rob Hunter

September Swim

New Poems
by

Rob Hunter

[handwritten inscription]

SPOON RIVER POETRY PRESS

Published by Spoon River Poetry Press. Orders to Spoon River Poetry Press, P.O. Box 6, Granite Falls, MN 56241.

Cover design by Niels Bolle.

Printed by Thompson and Shore, Dexter, Michigan.

ISBN: 0-944024-56-4

CONTENTS

for Nancy

I would like to thank Burr and Burton Academy and the Bigelow Fund for providing me the opportunity to travel to England in the summer of 2004 where I was able to work on this manuscript and where I composed some of the poems included in this book.

Vero Beach, 1969

Was it '68 or '69? I remember
standing on the beach and watching skyward
a white needle like a spark
crossing the blue bowl above.
Men going to the moon, I think I was told,
or going for a spin around the globe.
That was a squinting moment at 4 or 5.
Even now memory itself squints
at images so far off.

That rocket would drop pieces, or stages,
breaking the earth's gravitational pull.
I, too, have dropped stages breaking one gravitational
field, then the next, then another, speeding
forward. But let's not joke about our destination.
It's what's left behind that I'm focusing on,
the small blue planet of memory
wrapped in wisps of white clouds
getting smaller and more distant each second.

Those men came back,
dropping from oblivious black space
in a small cap with a parachute
right into the ocean,
green and blue back into sudden focus;
that's what I'd like one day,
fall out of my life into an ocean,
stand up in the surf, wipe my eyes,
and see myself clearly at five
with my parents and my sister
and not let one detail escape me.

Fish's Car

It was as gray as a bullet
before we painted it Canary Yellow
in celebration of its 300,000th mile.
1977 Buick LeSabre
fast as a bullet, too,
thirty-four tickets
in twelve states and two Canadian Provinces
to prove it.
Eight hot cylinders gulping
fuel like iced tea,
two hub caps, driver's side only,
a stuffed ferret baring teeth
on the back dash
with purple, orange, red, and blue
Mardi Gras beads around its neck,
a cassette deck that only played
Aretha Franklin,
and a hood ornament that could have been
Bo Derek complete with a Canary Yellow
string bikini
thanks to Dan Jette's steady hand.
Each ride in Fish's car
was my last:
power steering gone since '87,
tires as bald as baloney,
and Fish's impatience
which always made him pass.
I never cared:
If that car was going to heaven,
I wanted to ride the whole way.

Shape

Framed by my bathroom window,
my neighbors' stone cottage,
a good bit of their slate roof, some of England's blue sky,
and today, a single line weighted with wet laundry.
Included among pants, shirts, and shorts
is a splendid black brassiere

just like the one that you have.
It's gently swelling and swaying in the breeze.
I'm thinking of you, almost 3,500 miles away,
standing on your side of our bed
morning and evening
pulling on a shirt
or peeling one off
talking to me the whole time
about your day
or some student
or what the girls did while I was out,
and I'm staring at your black bra
considering the way it holds you,
the way its lines contrast with yours,
defining your rib cage and abdomen,
the straps your shoulders,
giving you a certain shape.

It's not just clothing that shapes us:
we are the sum of childhood,
parents, experience, places, people;
but lately I have come to doubt the influence
of any one of those things
because after so many years together
your hands still have power over me.

Far Above Mortal Issues

In one of those rare,
but strangely frequent moments
in our marriage,
we both awoke in the dark
of the night—
this time to the sound
of geese riotously passing
over our roof.
I imagined the V
formation barely visible against
the inky sea of night sky;

while anchored in the warmth
of our bed,
our legs twined together
and her left arm draped
over my chest,
I ascended on my own flight
of sleep,
far above the houses of mortal
issues, neighborhoods of
responsibility,
streets of feeling.

Kinship

He discerned it one day driving home from the dump
and he has seen it since on numerous occasions.
Even now in September, when the weather is warm,
he'll ride his bicycle from his neighborhood three miles,
past the other side streets with so many similar houses,
past the new construction—
dozens of homes for commuters on new crosscuts
cultivated on land that was forest
not twenty years ago—
towards the dump road,
itself the victim of sprawl.
"Where are people to go?"

Deliberately slow he peddles by
a low swampy area, an acre or two
of uncongenial wet land
a little too close to the landfill,
looking for that immense blue heron
that materializes out of the landscape:
a gray stump or some twigs come to life.
Seems like it's always there
whether he sees it or not,
like the wildness he still feels
in a distant corner of his heart
encroached upon for seventy-one years
that longs to spread wings and lift itself.

September Swim

Knee deep just feet from shore
your dive was more of an unhurried

fall, your hands ahead of you,
and then the water closed around your clothes,

your skirt collapsing suddenly
like a flower pulled by its stem through liquid.

You didn't make a sound.
The wind rustled leaves all around us,

and corrugated the water.
The sun dipped lower.

I didn't know if you would ever
appear again because in that split second,

standing on the shore of this pond
in the mountains, long afternoon shadows

were black shrouds on the water,
tinges of yellow and orange already

on some trees, I sensed the new season,
felt one season expire and pass on.

In that moment you were submerged,
swallowed whole; but like a loon,

you bobbed up and shrieked the cold
baptism out of your lungs. You then

stood up, wet clothes clung to your body,
your hands holding your surprised face.

Practice

The kids are at it,
little grown-ups,
going to work,
punching a time clock,
collecting pay. In high
school halls they hold
hands, make plans, kiss
good-bye. They're serious.
There are break-ups
and lessons, painful moments
to work through.

Smoking, a boy poses
while speaking to a
red-head in a car,
he leans in and laughs,
smoke envelops the girl,
but she's practicing too,
and laughs. Even that
other girl,
passed out at the party
and the boys who
raped her then
were practicing.

With Aloneness

I try to know her,
work to satisfy her:
she won't stay in bed,
but skulks through the cold stone house
all night—
          up stairs, down stairs,
a specter standing watch in the dark hallway
or rattling tea cups full of water
in the kitchen sink.

At each daybreak she's standing
at the living room window, back to the room
and me, as if to say,
          do something.
So I sit at my table
and attempt to fill empty space with letters and words.
When I see her thin shoulders convulse with silent sobs
and her bloodless fists knotting the material of her robe,
I don't dare say a thing all day.

Betrayal

April had to be kind
when the earth rolled like a heavy
sleeper waking,
the last dirty snow banks melting off,
sky clearing like a lake losing its ice,
air and dirt warming, softening,
rain cleaning the scum and debris
trapped so long by winter storms,
grass greening, buds swelling, birds returning,
days stretching out measurably—
nothing could stop the daffodil
from coming, or the lilac,
except the killing frost.
So common this time of year.

The Graveyard Shift Security Guard
at Westwood Lodge, Summer 1984
In memory of Anne Sexton

Evenings I patrolled the labyrinth of hallways
at Westwood with your ghost.
Because I was young, a college student doing a summer job,
you instructed me to lock away any thoughts
about the creatures behind doors as blank as death.

Outside Admissions I saw you climb into the backseat
       of a station wagon
where a woman foamed at the mouth.
You rubbed her shoulder blades
while her two adolescent sons stood outside the car,
pleading with her to come on out.

One night you gently caught that other woman in the hall
who lurched out at us, stripped to the waist,
her pendulous breasts unhinged,
each brown nipple like a single eye on a dumb swaying head;
you and a nurse led her back to her cage.

Every shift around 2 A.M., that time of night
when the new day felt just beyond dark trees
       at the edge of the hospital grounds,
I would feel you leave me.
The hospital quiet—
I couldn't hear the racket of nightmares then—
and nothing for me to do but shake off my own dreams
and make my rounds through dark buildings
and across lawns silent and dewy.

In Early March

Mount Equinox looks like a woman kneeling,
maybe breaking down.
The humped figure is shrouded
in snow squalls, half light obscurity.
It's like the image I see
when I can't chase her voice
out of my mind.
The woman who weeps
through the receiver
at the end of a curly wire
wants to die,
or rather,
laments that it was not her
instead of her daughter.
At 87 she wants to fly
from her own body,
be rid of skin and bone,
her very heart,
the agony they hold.
Death, like the promise of spring
to one mountain in a chain
that stretches so far.

Yard Work

What I started Sunday
had been waiting,
growing complicated
even before we lived
in this house.
An ignored corner
of the yard,
overgrown, like
a vulgar memory,
taking root after root:
nightmare bushes that snared
generations of leaves,
almost dirt now,
and trapped some
of the wind's orphans:
a plastic grocery bag,
a paper coffee cup.
Sap, blood, and sweat
bled from the work of saw,
hedge clippers and rake;
and try as I might
to make all look clean,
I've fallen asleep
each night since
acknowledging the green
roots' presence beneath
the wet spring soil.

Easter 2004

When I arose this morning
the world appeared unchanged:
what could I expect after death-
like sleep?

We made love under heaps of blankets.
Afterwards I brewed rich black coffee
and when it was done
brought a mug into the bedroom.
In the car I drove two miles for the Sunday paper.

Then, back home, reading all those thin black words
that transfigured themselves into rifle barrels,
prison bars, and burnt human limbs
did it seem so cruel to have to keep rising.

Rebecca

Her breast is gone
and she's shaved her hair
crew-cut style.
Standing near dancers she shivers
under a black leather coat.
What's to talk about
on a cool spring evening?
Her cheeks hollow
as if to speak,
but instead she remains silent
and pretends the occasion,
with its music and light
that penetrate the night
so insignificantly,
is joyous.

Losing Ed

I

I rake leaves,
speak with my dead,
work off the hangover
your news brought.
Gusts of wind bite with sarcasm.
The rattling and scraping of leaves
makes word sounds I strain
to decipher, suffer to believe.
More than others,
this particular autumn
mocks me,
the leafless maples, their stark gray branches
struck out stiffly against a solid blue backdrop,
my house's clogged gutters,
the early darkness.

II

We hang on developments
like news from some national disaster:
tests show the cancer is here but not there.
It doesn't matter—
the cancer *is*.

Placing a Stone

After 20 years
you must be able to find
the way back to your grave
after nighttime haunts,
travels back to places we lived or picnicked,
or even from my dreams—
sometimes I have the feeling
that you are outside on the lawn
looking in through my house's lighted windows—
sometimes you are the breeze taking my hand
or running like fingers through my hair.

After 20 years
a piece of granite engraved with your name
is for me.
That small weight of a headstone,
no less than the weight
of your absence,
is a blanket
so you might finally sleep,
and I have something real to walk away from.

Without
for Donald Hall

Using both arms
a fisherman at the edge of the surf casts off.
For a moment his line and lure are above
the water like a bird
he just released
before they plunge soundlessly into the waves.
He's working his way down the beach
walking sideways on wet sand,
his eyes on the water,
casting and reeling,
his body not registering the disappointment
of coming up empty each time,
but automatically coiling his body
back toward land, then snapping himself
and his pole forward
toward the water, hurtling
the dangerous hooks as far and as deep as he can.
The fisherman becomes a slow moving shadow
        down the beach,
still working at casting off
into the dark waves—
what we all do with less
deliberateness and hope,
ignoring our empty hooks.

Christmas Cards for the Dead

It's only after I finish
the names in the address book
that my mind turns
to the faces of those gone.
So I make out cards for them,
sign
all our love,
and print our names.
No long note, nothing heavy
to think about this holiday season,
just the picture of the family
and greetings.
There is now a second pile,
envelopes with only a name,
each one a granite headstone,
a small cemetery of my own.
I decide against postage
or a return address,
put the cards in the stack
with the rest to be mailed.
Confidently, I think of some Bartleby
in a nameless city,
in some windowless room,
sorting and destroying thousands
and thousands of dead letters,
occasionally opening one,
perhaps reading my salutation
to the deceased as he eats
his lunch of ginger nuts,
(a bad habit he picked up
at a former job),
and delivers my cards
to hungry flames,
the only way to reach the dead.

Saturday, June 7

The afternoon chugs in with clouds and rain.
Plans screech to a halt on their tracks.
There will be no digging dirt
in the garden, no edgework around the house,
no soaking up the sun. No reward of light
and warmth for the morning's hustle. The afternoon
feels like a long train ride. Nothing to do but flip
through old magazines, shift in my seat, get a cup
of coffee, close my eyes and listen to the sound of speed—
out the windows the startling wet green passing.

The destination of this day, the night station,
with another ride to known and unknown lands,
distorted desires, dreams of strange sequence
and misplaced faces. The pitch black tunnel of sleep,
the pinprick of light ahead.

Sunday School

Downstairs, brown and white floor tiles,
clean and cold and dustless.
The nursery with thin blue carpet,
red cardboard bricks, second-hand toys,
and children who weren't friends.
Then a chilly basement classroom, cookies for coaxing,
and Bible stories.
There were two distinct worlds
on Sundays, and I spent time in both.

Upstairs in the sanctuary, I'm a tiny being
looked down upon
by the unreal figures' pageant
on stained glass: bearded men in robes,
angels and lambs,
then the heaven of endless ceiling above,
and live men in white robes below.
Upstairs, even my small mother looked imposing,
standing and singing with a voice
I never heard at home.
And upstairs I'm suffocated by the air,
the pungent smell of a very old books
that had been left in a box in a garage or barn too long.

Fidgeting wasn't allowed, so it was hard on me,
especially in the warm weather
which is why once I learned
to pedal a bike I dropped out
of Sunday school spending those mornings
learning to fly or crash and bleed
under my own power.

Ritual

From a burlap sack
the boy's father pulled
them flapping and cautious,
hung them upside down
twine twisted around bony ankles.
Hard eyes blinking and wet
seemed not alive.
One of us in turn
would take the knife,
which we were instructed
to slide into its mouth
through to its brain.
All the boys agreed,
it was too easy—
they succumbed without a fight.
Their headless upside down dance
and the splattering blood
was grotesquely amusing;
the eggs we found inside
some of them made
one boy want to cry.

Consciousness

A boy emerges from the woods at twilight
into a ruined field, bordered by broken
stone walls, speckled with saplings, milkweed
        and bushy juniper,
where no crops have grown for more
than half a century,
and it seems strangely lighter, as if he just bought
another quarter hour of daylight;
brown oak leaves clamor in the wind
above him and before him a hard leaf
or two settles into the stiff grass.
The same breeze picks up his coat and his hair.
A hundred yards away a black crow
lands in the top of a deserted tree, caws twice,
and flies off into the wind, vanishes.
As he looks at his hands
it's not just the extra daylight
that makes the boy startle
when he sees flesh, bone, and vein,
but how it connects him
with generations of people
as ruined as the field
he is about to cross.

As a Young Man
Turk's Head Square, Providence, RI

Middle of the road.
Intoxicated.
Gawking straight up between gaping skyscrapers
The foggy night sky.
　　　Pigeons
fooled by the spot lights
between buildings,
fly in a false day—
now swim like pollywogs
in some mysterious quagmire,
squirm like sperm under a microscope,

at once weightless,
feathered wings riding currents of air,
up drafts and down drafts,
between the stone and steel exteriors'
plunging angles down to the street:

If they see beyond
the misty light to the black
wet street below
I am the figure frozen
wanting flight.

Ascension

It appeared like a god,
or a ghost—

a reminder,
standing on snow
in the floodlight's beam,
(it was the scream,
some animal shriek
that brought my dark face
to the window,
the light switch to my fingers),
a great gray owl,
temporarily blinded.

Nighttime predator,
I've dreamt enough
to imagine the moment
of being taken—
rush of noiseless air,
shock between talons

then a hop,
wing span
ascension
up into darkness.

Veins

I reach to the floor
to pick up something
as trivial as a pin,
focus sharply on my tanned
hand, the highways
of thick blue veins
and hints of metacarpals
like tent poles under
canvas
        and see
my dead mother—
her identical hands,

that rubbed my back
when I could not sleep,
that held her callused palm to my
forehead for fever,
that held me to her breast
for life,
that reprimanded,
that cooked, that washed,
that pointed to what I
should see,
        that did so much,

that I freeze for an instant,
not wanting to scare her off
like the nervous goldfinches
she used to lure
to our backyard crabapple trees
with a thistle seed feeder.

Boundaries
Buffalo Gap, SD

We've walked the whole east side
of the property pulling up rusted barbed wire
and reattaching it to posts. It's after
sunset as we make our way to the truck
across bumps of grass and crusted snow
when coyote cries fill the air. Their howling
and yapping sounds like it's coming from
every direction, blossoming up into
the darkening sky, then ceasing, leaving
invisible blooms to be traced with the first stars.

Back in the truck our headlights don't find
one animal as we creep over
the hayfield to the road. They're everywhere
and nowhere, slipping into the night
as if it were black water,
or ducking underneath ranchers' barbed wire fences
as if all those spiked knots weren't there at all.
That's the sad difference, I think.

There We Are

We're just down the bar
from the ladies still in their work
out clothes: they're cooling down
with some white wine.
Across from us a very fat
man and his small friend
are having the dinner special,
bloody slabs of prime rib,
baked potato, and the 24 ounce
mighty mug of lite draft.
They're watching the Celtics lose
above the bartender,
chewing with mouths open,
washing it all down automatically;
they look like they're giving speeches,
sermons, or a pep talk.
The waitress uses an empty table
to fold silverware into napkins.
She's getting ready for Tuesday.
Behind us several tables click
and clank with business.
To our left, the wall's big screen
screams with hockey,
fists and helmets, ice and blades.
While it's only Monday,
most seem reluctant to leave,
but at some point
the parking lot will drain,
headlights will pour off
in all directions
tracing the vacant streets
of town, moving through
the darkness undetected
like those solitary and hideous fish
that swim so deep in the ocean
they are never pulled gasping
into the day.

Journey

I almost expect to see a body
face down along the oil black and orange rusted rail tracks
among rank weeds, beer cans, chip bags
at the base of some graffiti scrawled concrete wall.
My greater fear is that the train
will not lock up its brakes with a scream,
that although visible to many,
not one other person
will say a thing about it, ring an alarm,
demand to stop:

that this train that departed from the green yellow fields,
orderly stone walls, and hedgerows bordering the square
        pastures
of the country-side ninety minutes ago,
will pull into the dark city station
like a prisoner of sleep,
and I will become one of them
moving along through the city streets:
it's worse because I don't see a body.

Night Vision

On Vermont 30 cutting northward
as fast as the curves and dips and rises will allow,
through summer dark toward home lights and family,
through a swath of dense forest,
moths, mosquitoes, fireflies, beetles, and various
        winged bugs
fill the nets of my headlights.
Their popping on the windshield
is so steady it sounds like rain falling.

Wipers and window wash won't help.
Night vision is tricky enough
without their smeared streaks further impairing my sight:
something much larger
might step into the road at any time.

Magnified moths as big as sparrows with cloth lace wings
swoop in from the blackness directly at my beams
to embrace that explosion of light and freedom
that they must have been searching for among
the dark trees, the shadowless stars.

Mid-Summer

Three
Lanky
Leafy
Sun-
Flowers
Grow
Lazily
Tall and
Green and
Yellow
Out of
The
Muck
Stuck
Rain
Gutters
Of my
Garage

Forgotten Flowers

I rummage trunks, boxes, dusty albums,
Negotiate my way around the dimly lit attic.
Sometimes I sift through days,
Parse the weeks for some kernel, some
Instant of irony or hope or failure or beauty,
Remembering, if I remember, they're all there,
All of those moments—so minute!—compressed,
Traveled by so quickly in the haste of my life, that
I am astonished to find a faded red flower in my thesaurus,
Odd thing I'd forgotten, its petals dryer than dragonfly wings,
Nestled securely between Last and Laurels.

Hummingbirds

We drank tequila last night,
my Mexican neighbor doing the
honors at the blender, and between frothy sips,
explaining the finer points of the liquor, of agave.
For hours we toasted the return of our friends
from two months in her native Ecuador
and ate grilled meat while all of our children
ran in and out of the house into the evening.

Despite the many salty edged glasses of margaritas,
I am up before the sun
feeling comfortable in a sweatshirt and shorts,
now sipping coffee outside
and considering how we come and go in life—
as fleeting as a tiny emerald hummingbird
that just buzzed to a halt
within an arm's length of me,
wings barely visible with motion,
its needle-like beak poised,
regarding me,
and in an instant, zipping away.

The July Garden
for my father

Tomatoes' tight green skin,
black prickled cukes,
beans lounge in the hammock of their shape,
and adolescent squash hide beneath
their own rainforest leaves.
The compost heap in the corner
heats and sinks to dirt.

It's no Eden and you're no Adam.
You toil, you labor.
You've loved and know loss,
your own Eve long since dead.
Your back aches after weeding,
and at night as you sink into sleep
your arch throbs the repetitious
turning the soil with your spade.

You're now in the practice
of planting winter rye,
a defiant patch of green against
autumn's dying colors, winter's inevitability.
I can see that it's not about hope,
we're both too old to listen to that lie,
but the beautiful pragmatism of the living.

Summer Daughter at One

Blackberries,
like little girls,
swirl with sugar
in the sun,
squawk in full red-black sentences,
and grow sweetest
in July.

February Robins

As we prepared to stay put,
there was no where to fly
from the blizzard swallowing the east coast
from Baltimore to Boston
and inland to us in Vermont,
you said you saw a flock of robins today.

I said we should open our doors
to the robins that arrived too early—
let them fly out of the snow storm right into our houses
Let them perch on the chandelier
above the dining room table,
on the TV, on the kitchen sink.
Let them zoom down the hallway
and from room to room.
Let them nest above the kitchen cabinets
and drink beakfuls from the dog's bowl.

Until we release them in a month,
when the snow is mostly melted
and the temperature mostly above freezing,
we might awake to their music inside our homes
instead of finding them in solid clots
of frozen feathers outside
and maybe for a month of our lives
we'd have challenged our own nature.

Cardinal

Amid warm seas

palm trees
Cadillac retirement

365 days green grass

a red splotch
in his backyard
one February morn

sends him to 65
years of Upstate New York
and with trembling
binoculars he tries to focus

Path

Moving one shovel-full at a time
in the floodlight's beam
a path can be made
in the early dark of the day

work against the night's work
a new foot of snow
wind heaping it in drifts
mid-thigh deep:

in the unfamiliar landscape
the cone of one light
a forest of sinister shadows
the house so far away
from the covered car and the covered road,
the task at hand
so critical
in the early dark of day

Stay at Home Mom

From upstairs windows
she sees the
the Green Mountains'
north south spine

and thinks how
it appears fractured
by the sideways snow,
the sub-zero temperature.

Winter Despair

There's a sheet of newspaper in a puddle,
the wind rippling it, the rain ironing it out.
From a distance it looks like a piece of old snow,
or ice, or perhaps I wish it were.
Near the neighbor's soaking cordwood
an upturned pizza box melts in the leafless bushes

At night, waiting for you in bed,
I can hear the water pelting the slate
roof above me, drum on the saturated
ground below; I can hear the sump pump
snap on, groan, spew out gallons more
from the basement: it will work all night.

New Year's Day

It just happened to be a Tuesday,
all of us home from school
still suffering the last long days of the holiday break.

We retreated from the house, the TV,
our rumpled beds, and the dishes in the sink,
went out for eggs and potatoes, bacon and pancakes,
and after we were full, for a drive

up the mountain, past the skiers on the ski slopes,
past the eight or nine buildings that make up the
        Peru town center,
and into the woods while
snow began to cover the road.

Not one other New Year's day
came to mind as the car made
fresh tracks, and the radio station faded
into the snow of static,

not one hard resolution burned to be accomplished,
not one regret quivered on my lips,
not one fear for what the future might bring
drifted into my brain:

the new snow lovely,
the kids laughing loudly in the back seat behind us,
the dog asleep in the way back,
that's all.

January Warm Spell

Too warm. The lawn seems to have risen to the surface
of the snow. And the snow banks, like ancient skeletons'
scattered bones, suggest a danger in nature. Near the house's
foundation, green fingers of daffodils three months early.

Against my better judgement, I too am getting spring fever.
The kids have it: they've been outside all day
without coats on, mud caked to their boots and fingers.
We open windows and turn off the heat, fresh air in the house.

I begin picturing myself building a patio out back,
shirtless and perspiring, handling stones and crushed gravel;
or of driving somewhere with my sunglasses on,
our little camper following us like a kite's tail.

Thrusting the bulkhead doors open I descend
the wooden steps, and out of the dark cellar
I drag the hoses and buckets. I wash the cars,
and then foolishly I water those poor green sprouts.

Winter Too Close, 9/11/01

Geese have been honking overhead
like cars in a hurry,
and even though it seems several weeks too soon,
leaves on some maples are turning;
the forecast is predicting nights
in the low forties later this week.
Lilies that a month ago stood so high and so strong
against any summer storm
surprisingly vulnerable in September—
they've easily been cut down.
We have prepared and lined up storm windows.
Each day brings fewer
minutes of precious light.
Signs of the fall are all around:
the smell of smoke and decay in the air.
The long winter that's coming
is what we prepare for now.

Fire and Ice

A scientist found
chemicals floating
in the atmosphere
prevent moisture in clouds
from condensing;
recent droughts,
wild fires
self-imposed;

meanwhile,
as pollutants warm
the globe, the frozen
mass above Canada
is retreating, melting away,
creating a northern
east west shipping route;
elated countries are
arguing over it
while the glass-like ice thins.

The Irony of Eating a Cheeseburger in a Roy Rogers Parking Lot off the Interstate While Observing an Eighteen-Wheeler Full of Cattle Pull Up

Too many large shaggy brown heads,
pieces of bodies visible through
the iron slats
a flank, a leg, ribs, a pink tongue, tails swishing,

one searching eyeball
peers between the metallic planks
at the asphalt, cars, pedestrians. Me?

On their glass like hooves they're dancing
their last dance, lurching to and fro
on the hard and once sanitary floor,
swinging to the music of the accelerator and the brake.

Chili

Leave the measuring cups and spoons
where they are, you'll need trust
for this one,
a recipe that's hard to do wrong,
and you will imagine and incorporate
your own variations as you grow more confident.
Roll up your sleeves, open a beer;
prepare to balance heat and patience.
Place your largest pot on the stove,
in it, a pound or more of ground beef
and the same of hot Italian sausage.
Use your sharp knife to slice
the sausages and remove the casings:
dial the heat to low.
Hear the meat begin to wake up
as you chop a green bell pepper
and a fresh jalapeno,.
cast them in on top of the meat;
now dice a big yellow onion,
sling that in too, but do not weep,
drink your beer.
Notch the heat a little higher.
Use the blade of your spatula to break up the meat.
Some garlic: 4, 5, or 6 cloves, whatever you have.
Mince them, toss them into the mix.
Listen to and smell the meat and vegetables
becoming something different.
Do not hurry this process:
this melding of flavors is not unlike
how we come to be wise in the way we incorporate
our experiences into present situations.
Remember that as you cook.
Drink another beer as you work the browning of the meat,
the softening of the vegetables.
When the meat is brown

crank the heat to high immediately.
Splash in 28 ounces of diced tomatoes
and three 14 and a half ounce cans of tomato sauce.
Heat is essential now: it created our universe,
it will make your chili.
Coax it to a boil. Stir with a long wooden spoon.
Now comes the magic,
which is no more than learning
to trust yourself:
sprinkle in some basil and oregano, just a bit,
black pepper and red cayenne; some salt.
Let your hand be surprisingly heavy with the cumin,
    scare yourself,
and chili powder to make this stew
the color of old bricks,
and add several splashes of tequila to the chili
and have one for yourself—you're working hard.
Two or three cans of red kidney beans, drained and rinsed,
(or beans you soaked for this purpose),
and the ingredients are complete.
Stir.
Observe.
Scrutinize the color;
see the different elements,
see the whole.
Perhaps you need more chili powder.
You can taste, but it is not yet ripe, like hard apples in August.
Let it boil and as it boils
reduce the temperature every couple of minutes
so you don't burn it.
Finally, when you've got it down to low and it's
    softly simmering,
let it cook for several hours.
Let your kitchen absorb the smell.
Let them who enter your door
know they are out of the cold.

My Finger on Your Spine

In the Harvest Moon's
wonderworking
luminescence
the Green Mountains' ridge
looks like
a nude
woman's spine, and I am
such a
colossus
in this lunar world
that I
want to
lie down next to her,
slowly trace
my index
finger along each vertebrae,
and by
seduction,
revive a landscape so close
to a six
month sleep
when
sudden southward geese
honking in the
darkness above
reduce both of us to nothing.

Remembering James Wright
North of Wheeling, West Virginia

On a hillside dense with beech and red maple,
high above highway 2
and the steel mills that define the Ohio,
directly across the river from Wright's
unchanging phantasmagoria of Martins Ferry,
there is a stone house:

no driveway leads there. Now thin trees grow
in the cellar
reaching for the window of open sky
where a roof once was,
their hard slender trunks pushing rotting lumber aside,
those same beams and boards
that once kept light and rain and snow out.

This day, not twenty feet from what was once
the front door are the remains of a wild turkey.
Its claws clenched, its feathered wings
spread out in supplication, or surrender,
its rib cage, which some predator picked perfectly clean,
makes the oval of a football,
stands like the white marble arches of an ancient chapel.

Offers

Each day they introduce
themselves like gentlemen
to my wife.
All of them well dressed, subtle,
showing promise.
Each one a suitor
willing to marry—
or carry on.
Each one expecting to seduce,
and all of them equipped
for at least that.
Each one wants commitment:
any of them would go anywhere
the minute she says go.
They want to buy her things,
any thing: secret panties, coats,
dinners out, hotel rooms, red wine
and the crystal glasses to pour it in.
They tell her it doesn't matter
if she has another.
They can be her "security,"
her "confidence."
"You deserve it,"
I heard one say.
But not Nancy. Nope.
Each one of those white
envelopes gets tossed in the trash:
no more lines of credit.

While Sleeping

Coyotes yapped, snapped, and howled
somewhere nearby, you recalled,
making a ghostly racket out there

in moonlight that was sifting through leaves
blanching the fields and houses and lawns
the color of photographic negative.

You were awake, fitful sleep,
and that's when you heard them.
Beside you, I breathed heavily and steadily,

my subconscious looting the unguarded
rooms of remembrance,
instigating bizarre dreams from closed books
of childhood's unremembered memory,

while those wild animals were raiding
Green Peak Orchard just up the ridge,

even more wild for the sweet apples
fallen, the dead of night, the silver light.

Another Day

The old man said there was another way,
a side trail, leading through a dense wood.
In the unfelt, unseen breeze,
ancient maples and oaks clash overhead
making human-like inhuman sounds;
on the ground, in dark places
on fallen trees and limbs and leaves, mushrooms and molds
work like slow acid, and now the fading footmarks
have turned, unexpectedly; so stopping
and glancing back, the familiar now out of sight,
the undergrowth closing in. Still, I pause and consider:
this path, though dark now, may bend back
to my intended destination, or may
lead to some precipice of the severest beauty
worth seeing. I decide on this day
to retrace my steps,
and swing homeward.

Acknowledgements

The author wishes to acknowledge the following periodicals where some of the poems in this book were previously published: *Veins, Fish's Car, In Early March,* Blueline; *The Irony of Eating a Cheeseburger...,* The Pittsburgh Post Gazette; *Summer Daughter at One,* PoetPourri; *Consciousness,* Indefinite Space; *September Swim,* The Cresset; *January Warm Spell, Practice,* Pegasus; *Boundaries, Vero Beach, 1969,* Small Pond Magazine of Literature; *Winter Too Close, Yard Work,* Blind Man's Rainbow; *New Year's Day, Forgotten Flowers,* South Boston Literary Gazette; *Without,* Pine Island Journal of New England Poetry; *Losing Ed, Saturday, June 7,* Free Verse; *There We Are,* Wind in the Timothy Press On-Line; *Ritual, Fire and Ice,* Manchester Literary Journal; *Placing a Stone,* Willard and Maple.

About the Author

ROBERT HUNTER was born in Syracuse, New York in 1964, and grew up in Attleboro, Massachusetts. Hunter received a B.A. from Hartwick College in Oneonta, N.Y., and a M.A. from Middlebury College's Bread Loaf School of English in Vermont. Hunter now lives in Manchester, Vermont with his wife and two daughters.